P E T E R H O F

S A I N T   P E T E R S B U R G   2007

HISTORY

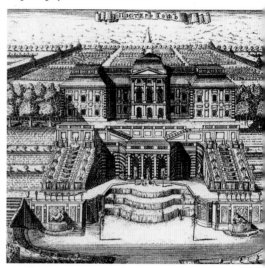

The Great Cascade and the Upper Chambers.
Engraving by A. Rostovtsev. 1717

Peterhof is one of the most famous suburban ensembles, sometimes dubbed "the capital of fountains", a majical sight of water and gold, marble and bronze, magnificent parterres and age-old trees. The residence was founded by Peter the Great at the beginning of the 18th century. By the middle of the same century it had grown into a gigantic ensemble impressing both Russians and foreigners.

The history of the ensemble dates from 1705, when the Tsar's snaw *Munker* put in to the shore of the Gulf of Finland at the place called Popovskaya (Pastor's) Grange. The vast island where Peter I was building the massive Kronslot Fortress was well observed from there. Soon a wooden palace (*khoromtsi*) was built here, "by the sea and by the grove", a little westwards from the present-day Marly. It was first mentioned in 1708. The first steps of turning the *khoromtsi* into an official residence were made in 1710 after the victory in the Battle of Poltava (1709). On June 6 Peter wrote in his daily "Journal": "His Majesty has deigned to observe the place for the garden and set the dike, the grotto and the fountains to be built in Peterhof."

The construction was started when the Northern War was at its height. In view of this, General Friedrich Wilghelm Bergholz, Gentleman of Bedchamber to the Duke of Holstein-Gottorp, wrote: "It's beyond understanding how the Tsar, in spite of the hard and prolonged war, in such a short period of time could build Petersburg, the harbours in Reval and Kronslot, a considerable navy and so many entertainment castles and palaces..."

The first architect of Peterhof is considered to be Peter I himself who personally made sketches and drafts by himself and gave orders to the Prussian master Johann Friedrich Braunstein. The latter arrived in Russia in 1713 together with his teacher, Andreas Sleuter, the court architect and the sculptor to King Friedrich I.

The construction was gained in scope after the series of glorious victories of the Russian army over Sweden, after which the Tsar made a diplomatic voyage to France. Duke de Saint-Simon then wrote: "Peter I, the Moscow Tsar, both at home and through whole Europe and Asia, has gained such a celebrated and deserved name that I cannot dare describe this great and glorious sovereign, equal to the greatest ancient men; he is a marvel of his century and a marvel for future centuries, he is a subject of eager curiosity of whole Europe."

Peter arrived in Paris at the beginning of May 1717 and stayed there till the end of June. De Saint-Simon mentioned that the Tsar paid special attention to the suburban royal residences – Versailles, Trianon, Chouzy, and Marly. On his first visit to Marly Peter "the whole day… was very busy… with the machine." It was famous Rennequin Sualem's mechanism, which supplied the Marly fountains with water. On his second visit to Marly the Tsar spent "three or four nights in pavilions." He was mainly interested in technical details of the system of fountains and parks and the architecture of palaces and pavilions.

By the time of the Tsar's return to Petersburg the eminent French architect Jean-Baptiste Alexandre Le Blond (1679–1719), Le Nôtre's pupil, had placed the work on a broad footing. He arrived in Russia in 1716 and was appointed the General Architect by Peter I. Together with Le Blond other French masters were working on the design of the Peterhof ensemble – the sculptors Nicolas Pineau and François Vassou, the painter Louis Caravaque, the metal master Guillaume Belin, the fountain master Paul Sualem and others. A great contribution to the decoration of Peterhof was made by Italians – the greatest sculptor Count Bartolomeo Carlo de Rastrelli, who arrived from Paris together with his son (later the prominent architect Bartolomeo Francesco Rastrelli), the architect Niccolo Michetti, the Venetian fountain masters Giovanni and Juliano Barattini. Prussian, Austrian, Dutch, Russian masters also worked in Peterhof. Among those were already mentioned Sleuter and Braunstein, the garden master Harnigfelt, the sculptor Conrad Ossner, the hydraulics master Vasily Tuvolkov, the architect Mikhail Zemtsov and others. By Le Blond's efforts about twenty workshops were founded in Petersburg which also supplied Peterhof: the workshop of decorative modelling (headed by Rastrelli), that of decorative wood carving (headed by Nicolas Pineau), of stone treatment (headed by Batalier and Cardssier), of foundry and chasing (headed by Sauvage).

Peter I.
Benois Coffre.
1716

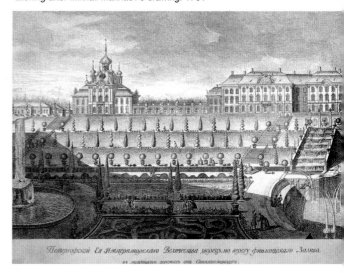

Great Palace, the Great Cascade and the Great Parterres.
Etching after Mikhail Makhaev's drawing. 1761

Le Blond himself headed the tapestry manufactory. The Lapidary Works was founded in Peterhof in 1725, the task of which was glass grinding and stone treatment for Petergof's needs. All that determined the speed with which the ensemble was getting its magnificent decoration.

In 1720 the works on the water-supply system construction were started in the Ropsha Heights, 24 km from Peterhof. It was a powerful hydro-technical construction, supplying all the Peterhof fountains with water. About two thousand people took part in the works headed by the engineer Vasily Tuvolkov. Those were mainly soldiers from the garrisons of Narva, Vyborg, Pskov and Petersburg. Already in the summer of the same year the Great Cascade, supplied by Ropsha water, was tested.

Under Peter's widow, Catherine I (1725–27), and under his niece Empress Anna Ioannovna (1730–40), only the works started by Peter continued in the Lower Park.

Peterhof flourished again under Empress Elizabeth Petrovna (1741–61). The great architect Bartolomeo Francesco Rastrelli then headed all the re-construction works in the imperial residences (besides Peterhof, those were the Winter Palace in Petersburg and the ensemble in Tsarskoe Selo). He widened Peter's Upper Chambers, finished the construction of the Upper Garden and attached the elegant Elizabeth (later Catherine) Pavilion to the Monplaisir Palace. Due to Rastrelli's talent Peterhof grew into a festive Baroque ensemble, a symbol of Russian Absolutism, which started its blossoming period.

The next stage in the history of the ensemble is connected with Catherine II (1762–96). Known for her rationalism, she didn't make any great changes in what had been built. She didn't make any serious repair works in the old constructions either. By the beginning of the reign of her son and heir Paul I the Peterhof fountain constructions had become immensely dilapidated. Huge reconstruction works had to be done. They were finished only in 1806, already under Paul's son, Alexander I. During this period such notable architects as Andrei Voronikhin, Carlo Rossi, and Vasily Stasov worked in Peterhof.

Architect Bartolomeo Francesco Rastrelli

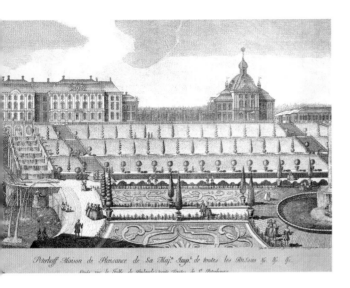

The accession to the throne of Emperor Alexander II (1855–81) was marked by the building of the railway (1857), which connected Peterhof with Petersburg.

After the First World War and the Revolution the Peterhof parks and palaces were nationalized and in May 1918 turned into museums. But the young government didn't have money for supporting them, and by 1923 the unique water-supplying system had almost gone out of order. The flood of 1924 made the situation worse: water from the Gulf of Finland flooded the Lower Park, washed away the shore, and filled the fountain pools with sand and silt. In 1925 the ensemble revival works headed by the architect A. Schwarz were started. By 1926 the fountains of the western part of the Lower Park had been reconstructed. Among them was the Sun Fountain which hadn't been working for more than half a century. By 1930 the walls of the Sea Canal and the Great Cascade had been partially reset up, the fountain water pipes had been changed, the overgrown parterres of the Upper Garden had been rebuilt after the drafts of the 18th century.

At the end of September 1941 after hard battles the Soviet troops had to leave Peterhof. Until January 1944 the town and all its ensembles of palaces and parks had been under occupation. Only part of the exhibits were evacuated. On the day of the seizure of Peterhof (September, 23), the Great Palace caught fire because of the shell which hit the Church Block. On the evidence of eye-witnesses, the Nazi forbid to put the fire out on pain of shooting. As a result one of the most beautiful mansions in Europe turned into ruins. On January 19, 1944, the day of the liberation of Peterhof, front-line correspondents recorded the horrible picture of ruin and desolation. The first reconstruction works were immediately started and continued until 1973. On August 25, 1946, and on September 14, 1947, the fountains were first launched.

Nowadays the Peterhof fountains, parks and palaces are kept in a great state. The collections which contain no less than 150 thousand of the exhibits continue to enlarge. Huge reconstruction works are continued too. There were already opened the Upper and the Lower Grotto of the Great Cascade, the Olgin and Tsaritsyn Pavilions of the Colony Park, and the Bathhouse. The Farm Palace and other unique monuments are going to be opened.

View of the Great Palace and the Great Cascade from the Sea (Great) Canal →

GREAT CASCADE

The Great Cascade is one of the biggest fountain ensembles in the world. It includes more than sixty fountains, more than 250 statues and reliefs. Water falls over the marble, tuff- and shell-faced stairways (8 m wide) and trickles down into a vast pool. The pool is decorated like a fairy lake with pagan gods sitting along its banks. The stairway parapets are decorated with gilt statues and fountains in the shape of vases. There are two grottos on the slope of the terrace between the stairways – the Lower and the Upper Grottos, or the Great and the Small, the interiors of which were designed to resemble natural caves. The adjusted and harmonious architectonics, the great number of sculptures sparkling with gilt, the richness of the facing, the power and variety of water streams make the Great Cascade the acme of fountain art.

The Italian cascade of the 17th century (for example, the cascade of the Toscana Garzoni Villa) lies in the base of the ensemble design. But the Peterhof Cascade excels all known prototypes.

Its construction works were started no later than 1715, when on January 24 Peter I placed an order "Of the next summer construction." One of the points of the document said: "To make chambers in Peterhof, also to dig out the canal from the sea... and to face it with natural stones... to make all the rest after the draft." Besides the draft a model of the central part of the Lower Park was given to builders. In 1716 Le Blond came to Peterhof and introduced some changes into the original design. He suggested to change the form of the central pool, making it in the shape of a scoop, and to widen the Sea Canal flowing from the pool to the Gulf of Finland.

Peterhof chroniclers have recorded the picture of the rapid construction process. According to the documents, already in February 1717, sixty big and twenty small lead gilt statues were delivered from Amsterdam. At the end of December 1718 Le Blond ordered flagstone for facing and in January 1719 he ordered sheet lead. In the winter of 1720 "lead figures from overseas" were additionally ordered (apparently after Braunstein's drawings). Then Conrad Ossner made models of decorative sculptures, reliefs, mascarons, and figured corbels after Le Blond's drawings. The metal originals were made after them in England. The casts were delivered to Peterhof in 1721–22. Another batch of sculptures came to Peterhof from The Hague in 1723, and in December 1725 fifty-eight boxes with marble figures were delivered.

Peter I hurried to launch the fountains in Peterhof by the celebrations in the honour of the end of the Northern War (1721). And the first test launch indeed had been made on June 13, 1721, i.e. 1.5 months before the concluding of the Nystad Peace (August, 30). In August 1723 the grand ceremony of the public opening of the Peterhof Fountains was

Vue d'un bassin de Samson, ces Jeux d'Eau, et cascades dans le Jardin Imperial de Peterhof

Dédié à Sa Majesté Impériale
ALEXANDRE I.
Empereur et Autocrateur de toutes les Russi

held. Bergholz wrote that Peter with foreign princes and an enormous suite came to Peterhof on 13 August, after the ceremonial meeting of the Boat of Peter the Great by the Russian Navy. The sight was really impressing. "We arrived in Peterhof about half past one. We immediately entered a splendid vast canal, flowing just in front of the palace. The Emperor navigated the flotilla by himself... Then all the ships, about 115, lined along the both sides of the canal. When all the people went ashore, the Emperor began guiding His Highness (Karl Friedrich of Holstein-Gottorp, the future husband of Peter's daughter Anna) and all the other noble guests everywhere, both through the garden and the houses. The fountains with lots of water were particularly good." On Bergholz's evidence, by that time the Peterhof ensemble had been fully built. "The splendid cascade is flowing over three ledges from the front side of the palace into the lower garden; the cascade is as wide as the whole palace, faced with natural stone and decorated with lead and gilt relief figures on the green field... The lower garden, through which, straight in front of the main block and the cascade, a stone-faced wide canal flows, is filled with parterres and beautiful fountains. The vast canal in the lower garden flows rather far, up to the very river (the Gulf of Finland), and it has strong dikes along the both sides and a harbour at the front end, which is enclosed with piled quay walls, behind which small ships can take shelter during the storm. The canal makes it possible to sail up to the very cascade under the main block of the palace, what is very pleasant and comfortable."

Bergholz completes the description with words of praise to Peter the Great: "... he has done the things, in which any other sovereigns can be hardly compared with, and if Russians nowadays don't fully appreciate it and are not enough grateful to him... I'm sure that their descendants will fully enjoy the fruits of today's reign."

Samson Fountain

The fountain was put in the centre
of the Great Scoop in 1735 by the order
of Empress Anna Ioannovna to com-
memorate the 25th anniversary of the
Battle of Poltava (1709). The water jet
of the fountain is the highest in Peterhof
(about 21 m). To supply such power
Sualem made a separate water-supply
system, laid from the Babigon Pond.

It's known that Peter I had a plan
to include a central fountain into the
ensemble. But his idea was slightly
different: the main figure was to be
Heracles "fighting with a seven-head
reptile called Hydra, from the heads
of which water was going to spurt along
the cascades." Whilst here it is Samson
who is taken as the main image, also
a very popular hero (in the 15th century
Samson Defeating the Lion was
a heraldic symbol of the Moscow
Princes). The choice accounts for the
fact that the Russian triumphal battle
took place on the memory day of
Sampson the Hospitable, the namesake
of the famous biblical hero.

The author of the original lead
statue was Bartolomeo Carlo Rastrelli.
In 1802, when the statues of the Great
Cascade were substituted, his Samson
was also replaced. The model of a new
bronze sculpture (3.51 m high) was
made by the greatest classicist Mikhail
Kozlovsky.

**View of the Sea Canal from the terrace
of the Small (Upper) Grotto.** →
In the foreground, Trumpeting Tritons.
In the background, below, the Voronikhin
Colonnades (Small Galleries).
Built at the beginning of the 1720s, they
were rebuilt by Voronikhin in 1800–03;
they got new facing of white marble
(about 500 t) in the 1850s.

Statue of Ganymede on the western cascade stairway.
Bronze gilt. Height 1.58 m. After an Antique original of the 4th century BC

Trumpeting Tritons Fountain on the terrace of the Small (Upper) Grotto.
Bronze gilt. Height 2.02 m. After B.C. Rastrelli's model (1720s – 1730s)

In 1799 Emperor Paul I ordered to replace the old sculpturs of the cascade by bronze ones. The most eminent sculptors took part in designing the models – Fedot Shubin, Ivan Prokofyev, Feodosy Shchedrin, Jean-Dominique Rachette, Ivan Martos, and Mikhail Kozlovsky. Part of the statues (in the view of the huge amount of work) were decided to be cast from the plaster copies of Antique and Renaissance masterpieces kept in the Academy of Arts. The cast and the installation of the new statues had been finished by July 1806. At the same time, the cascade balustrades were decorated with new vases made after Andrei Voronikhin's and Mikhail Kozlovsky's scetches or copied from the Antique originals.

Neptune mascaron on the terrace of the Small (Upper) Grotto.
Bronze gilt. Height 1.75 m. After B.C. Rastrelli's model (1720s)

Western cascade stairway

← ***Sculptures on the eastern cascade stairway.***
In the foreground, Amazon. Bronze gilt. Height 2.07 m.
After an antique original of the 4th century BC

Bas-relief "The Sacrifice" on the wall
of the step of the Great (Lower) Grotto.
Lead gilt, painted. 0.56 x 1.39 m.
After J.-B. Le Blond's drawing (1721–23)

Decorative vase.
Bronze gilt. Height 0.8 m.
After A. Voronikhin's
drawing (1801)

Sculptures on the western cascade stairway.
At the bottom, Fighter Borgheze. Bronze gilt. Height 1.56 m. Free copy of an Antique original of the 1st century AD

Terrace of the Great Grotto with the Basket Fountain.
In the foreground, statue of Jupiter. Bronze gilt. Height 1.84 m. After J.-D. Rachette's model (1801)

Bust "Spring" in the Great Grotto.
Marble. Height 0.74 m. Sculptor P. Baratta (1717–18)

Grottos

The Great (Lower) Grotto was built according to the design made by Peter I (with Braunstein's participation). Its outer wall is more than 40 m long. It's cut with five arching apertures and clad with tuff; the role of the key-stones is played by mascarons. In 1721 Peter I ordered to erect "a table with splashing" (trick fountain) in the central hall, and in 1723 he ordered to make "water screens" above the entrance (the project was realized by Peter Yeropkin in 1727). The beautiful Wheel Fountain was erected on the terrace in front of the grotto in accordance with the sketch made by Peter I. In 1860 the tracery of its spurts was a little complicated so that the fountain was named Basket.

The Small (Upper) Grotto appeared later than the Great, its project was suggested by the architect Niccolo Michetti. The works were finished in 1723. Along the outer sides of the grotto Michetti erected two fountains in the form of huge mascarons of Neptune and Bacchus (about 2 m high) belching forth water. There are also marble busts in small niches.

In the mid-19th century the Great Cascade was restored. The walls and arches of the grottos were reconstructed, and the gilt copies of Antique sculptures were set there.

Sculpture of Faun Barberini
in the Great Grotto.
Copper gilt. Height 2.09 m. After an
Antique original of the 2nd century BC

Interior of the Great Grotto.
On the left, Cupid and Psyche. Copper gilt. Height 1.34 m.
After an Antique original of the 2nd century BC

Fountain group "The Sirens" at the Big Scoop.
Bronze gilt. Height 1.38 m. After F. Shchedrin's model (1805)

One of the two Frog Fountains at the Big Scoop.
Bronze gilt. Height 0.29 m.
After a model by an unknown
master (1721–22)

The Volkhov Fountain at the Big Scoop.
Bronze gilt. Height 1.68 m. After a model by I. Prokofyev (1805)

Fireworks in Peterhof

Peter I founded a tradition to organize festivities with fireworks in Peterhof. The English traveller Nathaniel Reksol wrote in 1774: "The illumination in Peterhof surpassed everything I have seen before. In the arrangement of illumination as well as fireworks of all kinds, Russians outdid all European nations..." Nowadays this tradition revives.

GREAT PALACE

The Great Peterhof Palace is one of the most beautiful palaces in Europe. It's one of the greatest monuments of the 18th century and it is protected by the UNESCO.

The Palace represents a linear symmetrical baroque composition. The length of its main façade, facing the Gulf of Finland, is about 300 m. When seen from the Sea Canal the building seems soaring over the surrounding landscape. The cobble ground enclosed with the balustrade was built on the palace terrace already in the Petrine age. There is a wonderful view of the Great Cascade and the Sea Canal from there. Le Blond wrote about that panorama: "... these are such things which need to be seen in order to be estimated." The Great Cascade itself is designed to resemble the main staircase leading the Palace.

On the side of the opposite, southern, façade the palace borders with the regular "French" Upper Garden. The Palace seems shorter because of that garden, organically blending with the accurately lined landscape with large mirror pools.

The first period of the Palace construction, which had been called the Upper Chambers, dates to the 1710s. It was Johann Braunstein who started its erection, but he didn't take into account peculiarities of the terrace soil. That is why the palace started to subside and the walls cracked. In September 1716 Le Blond arrived in Peterhof and made the reconstruction plan by November. He was planning to strengthen the foundations, to build an underground aqueduct to draw away subsoil waters and change the lay-out and the interior decoration. Le Blond also demanded the extension of the doorways and window openings and the balcony in the Italian Salon (Picture Hall), which was "more proper for a better view than the balcony, where (only) four people can stand." Bergholz wrote about the interiors of the Petrine age: "The rooms are small, but not bad, hanged with good pictures and furnished with beautiful furniture. Among many pictures, there is one, a very big picture, which is placed in the house above the porch and depicts the battle, where Russians defeat the Swedes and put them to flight... the Tsar is greatly drawn and is very much alike..."

After Le Blond's death (1719) the palace reconstruction works were continued by Niccolo Michetti. The latter attached extensive symmetrical galleries to the sides of the palace.

With the accession to the throne of Peter's daughter, Empress Elizabeth Petrovna, huge reconstruction works were started in Peter's old palace in Peterhof. In 1745 the Court Architect Bartolomeo Francesco Rastrelli made drafts of a new building, where he retained the Upper Chambers as a historical kernel. Simultaneously he reformed the side galleries, ending in unpretentious pavilions. In the place of the latters he erected the magnificent Coat-of-Arms and Chapel Pavilions. On the side of the Upper Garden the architect "broke" the façade of the Palace with risalite blocks. He built the Main Staircase and the Light Gallery (the Dance Hall, the most luxurious room in the Palace) in the western block. Rastrelli adorned the interiors with

refined splendour. The main halls were decorated with suspended "mirror" painted ceilings. The abundance of gilding, mirrors and paintings produced the impression of a never-ending holiday. The works, started in 1747, were finished in 1756 and widely celebrated.

Since the accession to the throne of Catherine II (1762), Rastrelli was dismissed, letting other architects take the position. Those were mainly Jean-Baptiste Vallin de La Mothe, who had been invited from France as far back as under Empress Elizabeth to head architectural classes at the Academy of Arts. In 1766–67 in the Great Palace he reconstructed two rooms ajoining the Picture Hall in the west and in the east and decorated them in the then fashionable *chinoiserie* style. Another notable architect of the Catherine age was Yury, or Georg, Velten, who in the 1770s rebuilt some of the parade halls of the palace – the Avantsalle, the Throne Room and the Dining-Room. Those were the last most serious changes in the Palace, which, in spite of some interior changes made by Andrei Stackenschneider in 1847–50, remains the monument of the 18th century.

The main palace rooms, forming the official enfilade, are situated on the first floor, in accordance with "the court regulations." There are some official halls included into the enfilade: the Avantsalle (the Chesme Room), the Throne Room, the Audience Room, the Light Gallery (the Dance Hall), the White Dining-Room, the Picture Hall (the central hall in Peter's Upper Chambers), the Western and Eastern Chinese Studies, the rooms for secretaries and courtiers. Behind the official part the main rooms of the Private (Own) Part are situated. Only a small circle of people had the access to them. Those were bedrooms, personal Emperor's studies, dressing-rooms and salons.

Originally on the ground floor were placed duty and domestic rooms, and the white-marble entrance hall (Bergholz described it as "a splendid large *seni* entrance room with pretty columns"), with the Oak Staircase of the Petrine age leading to the first floor. The Staircase doesn't impress with either the dimensions or the decoration splendour. The great French sculptor Nicolas Pineau took part in its design and made masterly carved wood balusters. The big portrait of Peter I is exhibited there. He is depicted holding the baton and wearing the ribbon of the Order of Saint Andrew the First-Called. The portrait was made by the Dutch master Benois Coffre in 1716, during Peter's visit to Copenhagen (page 5).

Main Staircase

The interior of the staircase, which had been built by Rastrelli by 1751, is a hymn to the reign of Empress Elizabeth.
The sculptural decoration includes gilt statues, carved bouquets, caryatids, rocaille cartouches and other. Gilding is made of thin gold leaves of high standard that covered the carved wooden ground. Then they were either polished to mirror glitter or left untouched (depending on the effect needed). The tempera paintings were made in grisaille (monochromic) and pictorial (polychromic) manners. The wide coves of the "mirror" ceiling are painted with Cupids. The plafond (ceiling painting) represents the allegory of Spring (artist Bartolomeo Tarsia).

From the upper staircase landing through the doors with magnificent gilt decoration one can get into the Light Gallery (the Dance Hall) and through the narrow lobby, to the Blue Reception Room. The dessus-de-porte of the main doors leading into the Light Gallery is crowned with the sculptural allegories of Loyalty and Justice.

Allegory of Spring

Blue Reception Room

The Reception Room wasn't included into the main enfilade and served as a secretary's room. Here the so-called "daily journals" were filled, fixing the events happening in the life of the palace. The room is decorated by Rastrelli with smart solemnity. The walls are covered with blue silk, with gilt carved décor of wall wainscots, door and window frames, and the zigzag parquets (characteristic of Rastrelli's interiors) are made of palm, walnut and maple.

The western doors of the Blue Reception Room lead to the gallery which connects the palace with the Coat-of-Arms Pavilion.

Blue Reception Room

Chesme Room

The hall used to serve as the Avantsalle, which had been luxuriously decorated by Rastrelli in the same style as the Light Gallery – gilt carving, mirrors and ornamental painting. In the 1770s according to the order by Catherine II, Yury Velten replaced the Baroque decoration by the more restrained Classicistic. Only mirrors and "star-like" design of the parquet floor remained of the former decor. The twelve huge paintings, made by the German artist Jacob Philippe Hackaert in 1771–73 and hanged there in 1779, became the main decoration of the Room. Six of them represent episodes from the famous Chesme Battle of June 26, 1770, when the Russian Navy headed by Count Alexei Orlov, defeated the Turkish Navy.

Chesme Room

Night Battle at the Chesme Bay on the Night of June 26, 1770. J.-P. Hackaert. 1770s

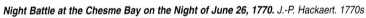

Dance Hall
(Light Gallery)

In the designs of all palaces Rastrelli used to include such halls lighted by enormous windows set in two tiers (the so-called double-lighting) and luxuriously decorated with gilt carving. Their prototype was the Mirror Gallery in Versailles. Compared with it, the gallery of the Great Palace is quite small (270 square metres), but the abundance of the mirrors and the large plafond of the mirror ceiling, representing Empress Elizabeth Petrovna as the patroness of arts and sciences (after Bartolomeo Tarsia's original), make the room seem larger. The magnificent parquet is made of maple, walnut, light and dark oak. There are sixteen tondos in the piers between the windows. They illustrate Ovid's "Metamorphoses" and Virgil's "Aeneid."

Allegory of Justice.
Sculptor I. Prokofyev. 1770s

Throne Room

It's the biggest hall in the palace (330 square metres). It was designed by Rastrelli as a hall for official receptions, concerts and balls. The walls were painted and decorated with mirrors. "9 dessus-de-portes decently called muses" by Lukas Pfanzelt were set in the piers. But in 1777 all that magnificence (except for the mirrors and parquets) was destroyed, and the hall was decorated by Yury Velten in the Classicistic style. The arch coves were decorated with heavy ornamental moulding; the walls were covered with reliefs by Ivan Prokofyev, Mikhail Kozlovsky and Arkhip Ivanov. The portraits of all the representatives of the Romanov dynasty, beginning from Patriarch Filaret and Tsar Mikhail Fiodorovitch, were placed in the piers.

Equestrian Portrait of Catherine II. V. Erichsen. 1762

Throne Room

The equestrian portrait of Catherine II, made by the Dutch artist Vigilius Erichsen specially for the Throne Room (1762), is exhibited in the hall.
The Empress is represented wearing the full-dress uniform of the colonel of the Semionovsky Regiment with the ribbon of the Order of St. Andrew riding the horse Brilliant, which she rode at the head of the guard regiments from Peterhof to take the throne. Contemporaries wrote that, "it is the most true to life portrait of the Empress."

Throne in the Throne Room. *Early 18th century*

Empress Anna Ioannovna.
H. Buchholz. Last third of the 18th century

Empress Elizabeth Petrovna.
H. Buchholz. Last third of the 18th century

Empress Catherine I.
H. Buchholz. Last third of the 18th century

There are copies of the portraits of Catherine I, Anna Ioannovna and Elizabeth Petrovna around the throne. The portraits were made by the artist Hienrich Buchholz to the order by Catherine II.

The throne is placed on a small podium, which, according to the legend, was ordered by Alexander Menshikov for Peter I. The throne is cut of oak, gilt and covered with red velvet. It has the double-headed eagle on its back. The feet bench appeared later, in the mid-18th century.

There is one more throne in the adjoining room, which belonged to Nicholas I. It is decorated with his mono-gram on its back.

Throne of Nicholas I

Audience Hall

The hall used to be called
Audience Chamber and served
for small receptions (audiences)
of Empress Elizabeth. It's one of
Rastrelli's masterpieces. The coves
are decorated with refined gilt paintings in
the shape of trellis netting (made according
to the special order by Elizabeth, who didn't
like the original paintings). The ceiling painting
(a copy from the work by Paolo Ballarini,
a representative of the Bolognese School)
illustrates one of the scenes of the poem
by Torquato Tasso "Jerusalem Delivered."

A beautiful collection of objects of decorative and applied arts is displayed in the hall.
It includes a musical clock "Venus and Cupid",
made by the Paris master of the second half
of the 18th century Gilles the Elder, Chinese
blue vases of "craquelés" porcelain, set in gilt
bronze in the early 19th century, statuettes
from the Meissen Manufactory, Russian
decorative vases of semi-precious stones and
others. The gilt chairs in the "Second Rococo"
style were made in the mid-19th century
for the Winter Palace in Petersburg.

**Decorative
vase made in bronze
gilt setting.**
Early 19th century

Illustration of the myth about
Dionysus and Ariadna.
Sculptor F. Gordeev. 1770s

White Dining-Room

This is one of the most elegant interiors of the main enfilade.
The present-day design was made by Yury Velten in the early 1770s. The walls are decorated with refined moulding. The oval medallions in the upper tier have bas-reliefs, made after the models of the most prominent Russian Classicistic sculptor Fiodor Gordeev. They represent mythological scenes with Dionysus and his beloved Ariadna. There are high ceramic stoves in the corners.

Since Elizabeth Petrovna's reign the hall served for solemn dinners and suppers. Nowadays the table in the hall is laid with a magnificent service made of "royal" cream biscuit. It was ordered by Catherine II in 1768 to the prominent English master Josiah Wedgwood and made at his famous Etruria Factory.

Wall and door panels of the Western Chinese Study

Ceiling painting in the Eastern Chinese Study

Chinese Studies

Western Chinese Study

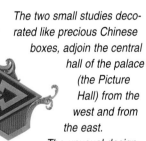

*The two small studies deco-
rated like precious Chinese
boxes, adjoin the central
hall of the palace
(the Picture
Hall) from the
west and from
the east.
The unusual design
made by Jean-Baptiste
Vallin de La Mothe in the late
1760s, is the tribute to the fashion
which had been introduced by Peter I.
The walls of the studies are decorated with original
Chinese screens with gold and silver painting on the
black lacquer ground. The panels are framed with
ornamental compositions made by Russian masters
imitating Chinese ones – as well as the paintings of
the ceilings, wainscots, window slopes, figured stoves.
The precious parquets are made of sandal, amaranth,
lemon-tree, ebony and orange tree.
The collection of Chinese and Japanese articles,
most precious Chinese furniture of the 18th century
(in the Western Study), and European articles in the
chinoiserie style are displayed in the studies.*

Northern balcony doors of the Picture Hall with the view of the Sea Canal

Picture Hall

Bergholz wrote about this room, the central one in Peter's Upper Chambers: "a splendid hall with a wonderful view of the sea…" This hall is really unique because of the view of the central panorama of the Sea Canal and the Gulf from its northern balcony, and the panorama of the Upper Garden from the southern balconies. In accordance with the inventory of 1728, under Peter I, the walls of the hall were faced with oak wainscots and the floor was paved with marble. In 1726 the ceiling was decorated with the plafond "Allegory of Arts" made by Bartolomeo Tarsia.

During the reconstruction of the palace Rastrelli replaced the cold marble floor by parquet and added the gilt carved setting of the windows, doors and mirrors into the interior. In 1764 after Vallin de La Mothe's design, the pictures and the wall-papers of Peter's collection were replaced by the then fashionable portrait sketches ("small heads") made by Pietro Rotari (1707–62). The collection of those portraits was bought by Catherine II right after the artist's death. The Picture Hall has 368 pictures set in the system imitating carpets. Rotari's "Self-portrait", placed on a decorative easel, is also exhibited there.

Dessus-de-porte sculpture.
After B.F. Rastrelli's design
(1740s)

Partridge Drawing-Room

The enfilade of the rooms, making the Private Half of the palace, begins with a small drawing-room called the Partridge Drawing-Room. It got its name under Catherine II, when the walls of the room were decorated with precious Lyon blue silk (brought from France) with partridges weaved among flowers and ears. The refinement of the design, the rich (32 tints) and delicate colour scheme are characteristic of the well-known master Philippe de La Salle. The old silk of the Partridge Drawing-Room has remained on the western door, in the window draperies and in the niche.

There is an old harp in the centre of the room. It was made in London by the greatest master of musical instruments Sebastian Erard (1752–1831).

Niche with the divan in the Partridge Drawing-Room.
Divan of the "Second Rococo" style was made in the mid-19th century

Niche in the Divan Room

Divan Room

Formerly it used to be one of the rooms of Peter's Upper Chambers (probably the room of Catherine I). Later Rastrelli made it a bedchamber with an alcove for the main bed for Empress Elizabeth. In 1779 Velten placed a small suite of furniture in the alcove and a wide Turkish divan beside the western wall. According to the legend, the divan was brought from Turkey and presented to Catherine II by Grigory Potiomkin. There are unique porcelain articles beside the divan – a refined vase of the age of Dmitry Vinogradov, the inventor of Russian porcelain (after 1756), and a porcelain figure of Zemfira, the beloved dog of Catherine II. The life-sized figure of the dog is made after Rachette's model. The walls of the Divan Room are covered with original Chinese silk of the 18th century.

Portrait of Elizabeth Petrovna as a Child.
H. Buchholz's copy of the mid-18th century from Louis Caravaque's painting (1710s)

Dressing-Room

The small but splendid room has retained its design made for Empress Elizabeth Petrovna. Only the furniture and the colour and the design of the upholstery are different. The latter was repeatedly changing during a century and a half. The silk, now decorating the Dressing-Room, was made in the 19th century after a sample of the 18th century.

Its design represents tightly arranged rocaille ornamental compositions with bunches of flowers on the cream ground. The wallpapers tone well with the refined gilt decoration and furniture.

There are portraits of Elizabeth Petrovna, Peter III and Catherine II on the walls of the Dressing Room. The equestrian portrait of Elizabeth Petrovna ("Portrait with a Blackmoor Boy") is one of the best of the Peterhof collection. It is probably Georg Christian Grooth who repeated his own painting of 1743 (kept in the Tretyakov Gallery in Moscow). The down to the knee portrait of Elizabeth was made in 1760 after the miniature by Charles Vanloo, one of the greatest Rococo masters, the Court Artist to Louis XV.

Empress Elizabeth Petrovna.
C. Vanloo. 1760

Empress's study

The interior of the study was reconstructed under Catherine II. The silk design (bouquets in baskets on the white ground) probably refers to that period. There is a study suite of furniture in the room, which was made at the well-known workshop of Georges Jacob (1739–1814). Among other "furniture masterpieces" are the heridon table made of mahogany by the French master Coulerue, the chest of drawers decorated with biscuit reliefs, which probably came from Benneman's workshop, the escritoire made by the German master David Roentgen (1743–1807).

The portraits of Paul I and his wife Maria Fiodorovna are presented in the small picture gallery of the room. The court-dressed portrait of Catherine II, made by Vigilius Erichsen, and the portrait of Elizabeth Petrovna, made by an unknown Russian artist of the mid-18th century, are also placed there.

Portrait of Emperor Paul I.
Unknown Russian artist. 19th century

Standard (Intercommunicating) Room

In the 19th century the room, known as Intercommunicating, was used for keeping banners (standards) of the Peterhof Palace garrison. Like all the household rooms, it hasn't retained anything from the original design. There is no information about the original wall upholstery either. At present the walls and the furniture of the Standard Room are upholstered with splendid silk with bunches of flowers on the green ground.

The museum collection has retained Luigi Premazzi's water-colour showing the bedroom of the Private Dacha in Peterhof, upholstered with that very silk. There is an allegorical picture by Jacopo Amiconi (1675–1752) "Peter I with the Goddess Minerva" among the paintings presented in the room.
The picture was made in the 1730s according to the order of the prominent man of letters and political figure Antioch Kantemir, who served as the Russian Ambassador in 1732–38 in London. Next to it, there is a chamber portrait of Elizabeth Petrovna, probably made by Georg Grooth.

Bedroom in the Private Dacha in Peterhof.
L. Premazzi. Mid-19th century

Cavaliers Room

The Cavaliers Room got its name because the guard of the Private Half was located there. Nowadays the furniture of European masters, the Chinese and Japanese porcelain of the first half of the 18th century are exhibited here. There are some battle paintings of the 17th century on the walls. The main decoration of the room is its design, made by Rastrelli: "zigzag" parquets, luxurious door framing, a large stove faced with tiles, elegant wainscots at the bottom of the walls, with gilt details.

Small Intercommunicating Room

This is a very small room, decorated with the luxury of a main room. The walls are upholstered with splendid silk of the second half of the 19th century, made at the Sapozhnikov Manufactory (Moscow). On the wall, the "Portrait of an Old Man" by Giovanni Battista Tiepolo (18th century) and the "Portrait of Vittoria Corombona", made by the Italian mannerist Scipione Pulzone in the second half of the 16th century, hang.

Large Blue Drawing-Room

The Drawing-Room served for dinners in the present of a small circle of people. That is why the main decoration of it is the tables with articles from the Banqueting Service for 250 people, specially made in 1848–53 at the Imperial Porcelain Factory for the Great Palace. The interior has retained the decor of the Elizabeth age, except for the ceiling painting made by Lorenzo Verner (1750). The magnificent gilt chandelier for eight hundred and six candles was put in its place. The cove paintings represent Elizabeth Petrovna's monograms, military attributes and flower garlands. There is a tile stove in the corner. The design includes French furniture of the late 18th century (the divan and the chairs), the dressers made in the style of Louis XIV by the most prominent master of the mid-19th century Barbidien, four splendid candelabra made by Saxon masters of the mid-19th century and others. The impression of solemnity is added by the official portraits of Catherine II and Empress Maria Fiodorovna (the latter was made by the prominent artist of the Sentimentalism age Elizabeth Vigée-Lebrun). The Drawing-Room got its name (Blue) in the 19th century, when it was upholstered with blue brocatelle (silk material, weaved with stylized bouquets matching in tone).

Portrait of Empress Maria Fiodorovna.
E. Vigée-Lebrun. 1800s

Candelabrum.
Mid-19th century

Catherine II,
the Legislator
in the Temple of Themis.
Copy of an unknown artist
of the late 18th century
from Dmitry Levitsky's
painting (1783)

First Room of the Reserve Half

Rooms of the Reserve Half

Second Room of the Reserve Half

The southern enfilade of the Private Half includes five small rooms, four of which were decorated by Andrei Stackenschneider in 1845–46 for the wedding of daughter of Nicholas I, Olga, engaged to the Prince of Württemberg.

The rooms, decorated with cold luxury, were stylized to resemble interiors of the 18th century with the furniture in the style of Louis XV and Louis XVI, made in the best workshops in Europe in the 19th century.

Table in the style of Louis XV with the tabletop decorated with Florence mosaic.
Mid-19th century

After Olga Nikolayevna's wedding the enfilade became deserted and was occasionally used, mainly as the court hotel for crowned visitors and people of high rank. It was then named the Reserve Half. Its main decoration is official portraits made by George Dawe and Christine Robertson, representing Nicholas I and his daughters – Maria, Olga and Alexandra. Prince Meshchersky wrote about them: "His Majesty Nicholas Pavlovitch could be justifiably proud of the unusual beauty of his three daughters…"

Third room of the Reserve Half

Fourth room of the Reserve Half

Crown Room
(Bedchamber)

The room used to adjoin the bedchamber
(the Divan Room) of the northern enfilade and served
as the main male bedchamber. It got its name (Crown)
under Peter I. According to his order a crown stand was
placed there.

There is an alcove in the northern wall of the room, at both sides of
which the doors lead to the Divan Room. The room is upholstered with
original Chinese silk of the 18th century, painted with water colours
(the scenes represent the process of porcelain making at the Imperial Factories
in Ching-te Shen). The furniture of the room includes a splendid gilt bed of the
18th century made by South German furniture-makers and a magnificent
chair-closet.

Italian heridon table with the mosaic marble tabletop.
18th century

Oak Study

The Oak Study is the only one in the palace interiors which has almost fully retained the design of the Petrine age. The study is known to be designed by Le Blond himself and that it was he who suggested decorating it with wainscots with subject carving, "because monotonous wainscots are boring for the eyes."

In 1721 Bergholz wrote about this room: "An especially remarkable place is the study where the Tsar's small library is placed, consisting of different Dutch and Russian books; it is decorated by a French master and notable for its splendid carving." It is almost the same now, only with some slight changes.

Detail of the panel with the depiction of Turkish trophies

Cupboard in the Intercommunicating Room near the Oak Study.
Late 17th – early 18th centuries

Coat-of-Arms Pavilion

The pavilion was built by Rastrelli in 1745–55. It got its name due to the Coat-of-Arms of the Russian Empire crowning the cupola. The huge figure is made so that spectators can see the double-headed eagle under the crown from everywhere. The cupola carving was made under the guidance of the master Stahlmeier in 1751.

Silver frame with a portrait of Peter I.
Master S. Boit. 1717

Snuff-box "Peterhof."
Master G. Wigström. The Fabergé firm. 1909

Study

Bedroom

Dressing-Room

In the 1750s the rooms of the pavilion were given to Grand Duke Peter Fiodorovitch and his wife Catherine Alexeyevna. When Catherine became Empress, she turned the pavilion into the guest one. Nowadays the reconstructed interiors present jewelry of the Peterhof collections (the Special Storeroom).

Chapel Pavilion (Palace Church of Apostles Peter and Paul)

Designing the reconstruction of the Upper Chambers, Rastrelli included the Chapel Pavilion into the ensemble. The pavilion, crowned with five cupolas (according to the wish of Empress Elizabeth) and containing the altar consecrated to the Apostles Peter and Paul. The cupolas of the block are luxuriously decorated with carving, made in 1749 under the supervision of the master Girardon.

The church is famous due to the fact that the children of Emperor Nicholas II, born at the Lower Dacha at Alexandria, including Tsarevich Alexei, were baptized there.

Interior of the Church of Peter and Paul in the Chapel Pavilion. E. Gau. 1842 →

View of the Chapel Pavilion from the eastern Square Pond

PETERHOF PARKS

At present the Peterhof ensemble of parks and palaces occupies more than a thousand hectares. There are about fifteen parks stretching ten kilometres along the Gulf of Finland. The Lower Park is the main one (area – 102.5 ha – 2.5 x 0.5 km), the masterpiece of the landscape architecture. Pietro Gonzaga wrote about it: "The shooting fountains, splendid symmetrical cascades, reservoirs, surrounded by nymphs, tritons and other sea deities, fantastic grottos, planned with whimsical irregularity… surrounded by balustrades hanging terraces with vases full of flowers, statues, busts, etc. And at last, this regularity, artificially gracious, noble, soul-elevating…"

Bergholz said, that under Peter the Great the park was already "surrounded by lots of beautiful and merry avenues… The two biggest of them on the both sides of the garden lead through the grove to the two entertainment palaces (the Hermitage and the Monplaisir), situated on the same distance from Peterhof and by the very Neva… to the right… Monplaisir is placed; there are a lot of splendid bushes, avenues and parterres in its garden, a large pond faced with stones, in which swans and other birds are swimming, a special house for small birds and other various entertainment things… So Peterhof consists of four separate gardens, surrounded by pleasant places with groves and water, and all of them are connected with one another."

The described by Bergholz "beautiful and merry avenues", groves and parterres were planted in the flat low place, which had formerly been the shelf of the ancient Litorina (Periwinkle) Sea and by the beginning of the 18th century had had quite poor vegetation. All the tree abundance of the park is hand-made. According to the order by Peter I, tens of thousands of saplings were brought from the districts near Moscow, Pskov, Siberia, Crimea, Sweden, Holland, Poland and others. While staying abroad in 1717, Peter made "the drafts for the Peterhof garden with notes of my own opinion", where he mentioned all the buildings, arbours, parterres and bird houses in detail. The Tsar also remarked: "To thin the groves out, to plant thicker trees in the places of poor forest, and to plant thinner trees near the slanting road from the chambers to Monplaisir, and to cut them no higher than 12 feet to make the cutting time more convenient and thus to help the gardener in time… To try to get clay out of the groves not to make more trees die." Peter's closest helper in the park creation was the Dutch garden master Leonard van Harnigfelt.

Nowadays the fountains of the Lower Park have no comparison in the number (about two hundred), the joint power and the height of water jets and partially in the engineer solution. They function daily from May to October all day long. This "diligence" is supplied by the unique water system from the Ropsha Heights, constructed by Peter I in 1720–21. In the daily journal of Peter I it's recorded, "… on August 8, 1721. His Majesty and Her Majesty the Empress were pleased to visit Peterhof; it was reported on that very day that the canal from the Kavasha River past the Ropsha Grange has been already dug out for 20 versts…" After that Peter accompanied by his wife Catherine, Karl Friedrich of Holstein-Gottorp, the foreign ambassadors and the suite went to Ropsha, where he himself let the

water go through the new water-supply system. On the historians' evidence the water had reached Peterhof "by the next morning, at 6 o'clock and then all the fountains and cascades were launched." The abundance of Ropsha water urged on buil-ding new fountains. In 1721 the Bowl Fountains (Italian and French) were opened, in 1722, the Adam Fountain was launched on the terrace cascades (on the slopes of the terrace along the sides of the Great Cascade). In 1723–24 the fountains of the Small Galleries attached to the Great Cascade, the Ménager Fountains and the Cloche Fountains in Marly, the fountain in the Menazherny Pond, the Pyramid Fountain, the Dragon Cascade (formerly the Ruin Fountain) began to work. In the 1720s the project of the Golden Hill Cascade and the Orangerie Fountain was started.

So, most of the fountains of the Lower Park were constructed under Peter I. They are the monument of his indefatigable energy.

The further development of Peterhof did not change the Lower Park a lot; just a few fountains were added. In the second half of the 1720s – 1730s the Triton Fountain was erected in front of Peter's Orangery, the Favourite Fountain (after the example of the Versailles fountain) was built behind the western gallery beside the Scoop Pool and the construction of the Eve Fountain was finished. The Golden Hill and the Chessboard Hill Cascades and the Pyramid Fountain were decorated, the Roman Fountains and the Whale Fountain were built. Under Catherine II the Birch Walk (after B. Fok's design) was made. Under Paul I the Pyramid Fountain, the Great and the Small Grottos of the Great Cascade were surrounded by marble balustrades; the stone wall was built on the eastern border of the Lower Park and others. Under Nicholas I (1825–55) the Lower Park got a row of "historical" stylizations – the Lion Cascade in the form of a Greek temple; the fountains of the Marble Benches (Danaide and Nymph), the landscape parks, such as Alexandria, Colony and Meadow were founded. The fountain avenues were made along the Great (Sea) Canal, which had lost its purpose of the main entrance to the Palace for ships. The works on facing with marble of the existing constructions – the Terrace Cascades, the Voronikhin Colonnades, etc, were continued. Under Alexander II (1855–81) works in the Lower Park were completed mainly in the Monplaisir, where the cosy Chinese Garden appeared.

Simultaneously the character of the park was changing. Under Peter the Great it used to be private, and in the 19th century it got the public status. There were held celebrations and festivals which became especially crowded after the opening of the railway (1857).

Great Parterres of the Lower Park with the French and Italian Fountains (to the right, in the background) →

French Fountain of the Great Parterres

Great Parterres and the Orangery Garden

Orangery Block

The Great Parterres are vast, regular flower parterres, symmetrically placed at the foot of the Great Cascade. They had been made by 1721, when in the centre of the both round pools (25.5 m in diameter) with powerful fountains spurting from huge bowls were built after Niccolo Michetti's design. The western fountain got its name (Italian) because its hydrotechnical system had been constructed by the Italian brothers Barattini, and the eastern one got its name (French) because it had been constructed by the Frenchman Paul Sualem. Originally the bowls were made of oak. In 1854 the bowls were cut out of Carrare marble at the Peterhof Lapidary Works (the weight of each is 17 t).

To the east of the Parterres a short avenue leads to one more garden of the Petrine age – the small Orangery Garden. Its main decoration is the Triton Fountain in the pool which is 15 m in diameter (1726). The sculpture of the fountain (Triton fighting with the sea monster and turtles) was made after B.C. Rastrelli's design. To the north the garden is surrounded by the block of the Great Orangery (the façade is 34 m long), built by Braunstein and Zemtsov in 1722– 25. The building was used for keeping pots with exotic plants in winter.

Triton Fountain in the Orangery Garden

Turtle of the Triton Fountain

Pyramid Fountain

It's one of the most spectacular fountains in Peterhof. It stands some-what separately in the Lower Park, apart from the lively paths. The first records about it were made in 1721, when it was called "a water pyramid with small cascades."

The fountain was designed by Niccolo Michetti, who, according to the order by Peter I, used Mansart's Versailles Obelisk Fountain as a model. But the master Paul Sualem made 505 sprayers in the fountain, that is twice as many as in the Obelisk Fountain. It turned the Pyramid into the tight, compact and at same time light water pillar. Originally the pool and the steps of the fountain were made of wood and faced with gilt lead; the grass parterre was surrounded by the wooden balustrade.

In 1799, after the design of the architect I. Yakovlev, the fountain got it marble "framing."

Chessboard Hill and the statue of Peter I

Northwards from the Pyramid a small path leads to the wide Marly Avenue. The bronze statue of Peter I on a high granite pedestal stands on its crossing with the Monplaisir Alley. It was cast after the design of the most prominent Russian sculptor of the second half of the 19th century, Ivan Antokolsky and erected in 1884. Southwards from the statue the Dragon (or the Chessboard) Hill Cascade can be viewed. It's descending to the vast parterre, from which alleys diverge to the all greatest ensembles in the Lower Park. On the way from the statue of Peter I to the parterre the surprise fountain Water Path with 300 sprayers (after Niccolo Michetti's design, 1721) is placed.

The construction of the Chessboard Hill Cascade was started under Peter the Great. Originally when there was no cascade yet, its grotto already existed. It was then called Small and was one of the first constructions in the park. In 1721, after Michetti's design, the construction of the cascade was started. It was made in the form of the slope of tuff, on the sides of which ruined towers were placed (hence its first name – Ruin Cascade). Already in 1737 the alterations in the decoration of the cascade started. After Blank's design the cascade got the discharge out of four wide steps. In January 1739 three brightly couloured dragon figures (the sculptor Conrad Ossner) were put at its upper grotto. In the mid-18th century the cascade steps were painted to resemble a chessboard. After that it was called both the Dragon and the Chessboard Hill.

← *Panorama of the Parterre Garden in front of the Chessboard Hill Cascade and the Roman Fountains*

View of the eastern Roman Fountain from the Chessboard Hill Cascade. *In the foreground, one of the marble sculptures of the cascade*

Roman Fountains

The two grand double-tier fountains, erected in 1739, are situated in the Parterre Garden in front of the Chessboard Hill. The architects Blank and Davydov rendered with some changes, the famous fountains in the Square of Saint Peter in Rome – slightly heavy, but remarkable in their architecture. In 1763, after Rastrelli's design, the fountains were moved to the line of the then made Birch Walk, where two new pools were built for them. Under Emperor Paul I (1798–1801) the fountains were rebuilt in granite and marble with the same architectural forms. In 1817 their lead mascarons were replaced by the bronze ones, cast after Ivan Martos's models.

Mascaron on the Roman Fountain

Adam and Eve Fountains →

Westwards from the statue of Peter I the long (2 km) Marly Avenue goes from the eastern border of the Lower Park to the Marly ensemble. In 1721 the construction of the pair fountains, representing the primogenitors of the Mankind, Adam and Eve, was started in the avenue. The marble sculptures were made in Venice by the sculptor Giovanni Bonazza in 1718, according to the order by Peter I. They are set in the centre of the eight-sided pools (17 m in diameter); sixteen high jets spurt out of the pedestal feet. The fountains are placed on the crossing of the eastern and western parts of the Lower Park, on the same distance from the Sea Canal, forming the focal point of the park composition.

Adam and Eve Fountains on the Marly Avenue

← *Sun Fountain*

The fountain is placed in the centre of the large pool
(70 x 30 m), included into the ensemble of the Ménagerie Garden.
The author of the design was Niccolo Michetti (1724). In the
1770s Velten made the original construction of the fountain more
complicated. Now its central fountain is represented by the column
(3.5 m high), on the peak of which the double gilt disc is set.
Water jets spurt around the disc. The column rolls with the help
of the water wheel hidden in the pedestal.

Oak-tree. Sculptor B.C. Rastrelli. 1735.
Erected in the Lower Park in 1802

Favourite Fountain.
Architect M. Zemtsov, sculptor C. Ossner. 1725

Trick fountains

The trick fountains were brought into fashion by Peter I
from abroad, where they were popular with the court
of Louis XIV. Nowadays the trick fountains of the 18th century,
functioning only in Peterhof, are one of the most favourite
entertainments for visitors.

One of the Bench Trick Fountains in the Monplaisir Garden

Mushroom (Umbrella). Architect F. Broyer. 1796

Cupola of the Eastern Aviary

Ménagerie Garden and the Aviaries

The Garden was made in 1717–24 as a ménagerie analogical to the one Peter I had seen in Versailles. In 1722 two pavilions of the Aviaries were set here. From the outside the pavilions are decorated with oyster shells and tuff, and inside they have refined tempera paintings, made in 1721 by the prominent French artist Louis Caravaque. Nowadays, as well as under Peter I, birds are kept here.

View of the Eastern Aviary from the Swan Pond

Sheaf Fountain, the central fountain of the Monplaisir Garden

Catherine Pavilion

Monplaisir

The Monplaisir Palace (from French "mon plaisir" – my pleasure) is the first Peterhof ensemble of palaces and parks. Its construction is connected with the order of 1709 placed by Peter I, according to which "entertainment palaces of stone architectural work" were to be built in Peterhof. The draft of one of those palaces had been already made by the Tsar by 1711. Although the construction works began only in 1714, when Peter made the draft with the inside design of the Monplaisir Palace.

In front of the southern façade of the palace by 1724 the garden had been laid out. The first two Bench Trick Fountains in Peterhof, entertaining the Tsar, his guests and the suite, were placed at the exit of the garden. Already in the age of Elizabeth Petrovna the elegant "entertainment palace" (the Catherine Pavilion) was included into the Monplaisir ensemble.

Psyche Cloche Fountain

View of the Bathhouse from the ménager fountain of the Chinese Garden

Monplaisir Garden

The garden is probably the smartest of all the gardens in Peterhof. It is divided into four parterres, which join in the central ground with the picturesque Sheaf Fountain (Mikhail Zemtsov received the order of its construction from Peter I in 1724).

In the centres of the parterres the cloche fountains were placed (from French "cloche" – bell; in such fountains water streams over bell-shaped surfaces). There are gilt sculptures on the fountains: Apollino, Faun with the Kid Goat (the bronze copies from Antique originals), Bacchus (copy from Sansovino's original) and Psyche (copy from Antonio Kanova's original).

Bathhouse

The Bathhouse is a refined building standing eastwards from the Monplaisir Palace. It used to be Peter's wooden bathhouse (Mylnia), which was repeatedly reconstructed and comforted.

Under Elizabeth Rastrelli built the Assembly Hall and the Kitchen attached to the Bathhouse and a new bathing hut. Under Catherine II in the place of Elizabeth's bathing hut a swimming pool was built with a lifting bottom, with the help of which water came into the pool from the Gulf of Finland. In 1865–66, according to the order by Alexander II, the architect Eduard Gan rebuilt the Bathhouse in stone, retaining the old design of the façades and the row of rooms of the 18th century. There appeared a few new smart rooms in the building, and halls for water treatments. Simultaneously at the eastern façade of the Bathhouse the tiny Chinese Garden was laid out. It got its name due to its specific design in the Chinese-Japanese style.

Parterre of the Monplaisir Garden with the fountain "Faun with the Kid Goat" →

Shell Cascade in the Chinese Garden

City Landing-Stage. A. Stork. 1690s

Gallery of Monplaisir

Monplaisir Palace

Bergholz said that it was the Monplaisir Palace, "the small but cute house, which is specially decorated with a great number of wonderful Dutch paintings", where Peter stayed during his visits to Peterhof, "here he is absolutely in his sphere and that is why he gave this place the name of 'my pleasure'."

The palace is one-storeyed, with the floor on the same level with the ground. It was built by Peter as a merry stylization of a rich Dutch house. Its central block (the Palace) includes seven rooms: the Main Hall and the adjoining rooms – the Maritime Study, the Bedroom and the Secretary's Study to the west, the Pantry, the Kitchen and the Lacquer Study, to the east. In 1717 the glazed galleries (each is 22 m long), ending in small pavilions – Lusthaus Pavilions (German "Lust Haus"), were built. The Lacquer and Secretary's Studies were placed on the same axis with the galleries and the interiors of the Lusthaus Pavilions, making the enfilade look smart.

Main Hall

MONPLAISIR PALACE

Door panel of the Lacquer Study

Lacquer Study

The ornamental works of the Monplaisir rooms were held in the 1710s – 1720s. The decoration has lots of facing with wainscots of waxed oak and ceramic tiles, paintings made after Philippe Pillement's drafts by masters of the Armoury. The floors are covered with parquet of black and white marble slabs, made to resemble a chess-board. The collection of paintings in the Monplaisir Palace became the first picture gallery in Russia. Under Peter I it included 201 canvases by Dutch, Flemish and Italian masters of the 17th – early 18th centuries. By the summer of 1719 Braunstein had prepared the project of a "Lacquer Chamber" with the decor in the Chinese style for Monplaisir. Ninety-four lacquered panels, decorating the room, were brought to Peterhof in February, 1722. Russian masters made filigree painting on them, representing Chinese landscapes and scenes from Chinese life. The study is decorated with a collection of precious Chinese porcelain.

Maritime Study

Kitchen

Secretary's Study

Catherine Pavilion

The Pavilion (originally the Elizabeth Pavilion) was built by Rastrelli in the place of the old Monplaisir orangery in 1748–49 which under Empress Elizabeth Petrovna was used as an "entertainment" one. Dances, concerts, masquerades, card games were held here. Since the accession to the throne of Peter III (1762), his wife, Catherine Alexeyevna, was living there. On June 29, 1762, she moved to Petersburg from the Palace and was announced the Empress. In 1785–86, according to the order by Catherine, Giacomo Quarenghi, with the assistance of the sculptor Rachette and the artist Scotti, fully reconstructed the interiors of its eight rooms in the Classicistic style.

The Yellow Hall is the most solemn room in the Pavilion. There are official portraits of Catherine II on the walls (the copy of the early 19th century from the portrait by Johann-Baptist Lampi the Elder) and Alexander I (1825, the artist George Dawe). The main decoration of the hall is the items from the Guryev Service, ordered in 1809 to the Imperial Porcelain Factory, then headed by Count Guryev. The service, which had been made till the late 19th century, is one of the biggest (about five thousand items) and the most famous porcelain sets. Its paintings and sculptural design, made after the models of the prominent sculptor Stepan Pimenov, present the so-called folk types.

Items from the Guryev Service.
Porcelain, overglaze polychrome painted, gilt

There is also a tapestry exhibited in the hall, made according to the order of Napoleon, after Steiben's painting, illustrating the scene of Peter I rescuing fishermen during the storm on the Lake Ladoga. The work on the tapestry was finished after Napoleon's dethronement, after which Louis XVIII presented it to Alexander I.

Other rooms are not so magnificent, but smart and elegant. They are decorated with mouldings and paintings, with expensive furniture specially made for Peterhof in the late 18th – early 19th centuries after the design of the most prominent architects – Carlo Rossi, Andrei Voronikhin and Vasily Stasov.

Green Reception Room

Study of Alexander I

Console in the Egyptian style.
Early 19th century

Hermitage Pavilion

Surrounded by the wide ditch with water, with the lift-bridge over it, "the entertainment palace" Hermitage is one of the many projects of Peterhof made under Peter the Great. The palace stands symmetrically to Monplaisir, westwards from the Sea Canal, by the shore of the Gulf of Finland. It was built after French "hermitage" examples (from French "ermitage" – a hermit's shelter), which were very popular in the 17th – 18th centuries. The peculiarity of such palaces became the arranging of the kitchen on the ground floor and the dining-room on the first floor, where meals were served with the help of the special lifting system in order not to spoil the intimacy of the dinner with servants' presence.

Oak Staircase

Kitchen

Pavilion Hall (Dining-Room) of the Hermitage

The design of the Peterhof Hermitage, prepared by Braunstein, was approved by Peter I in January, 1721. The works on the building and decoration had been held till 1725, when the last "strokes" were made: the oak balconies were decorated with hammered railings, copied from the Imperial Flemish ship "Ingermanlandia", the lifting system for meals serving was constructed, the table was placed in the Pavilion Hall, occupying the whole upper floor of the pavilion. The Lower Park and the Gulf of Finland can be seen through the high (beginning just from the floor) windows of the hall.

Battle of Poltava.
Copy by an unknown artist of the 18th century
from a painting by Ivan Nikitin (1727)

The alley going north-west-wards from the Hermitage brings us back to the Great Parterres. At their northern borders in thick brushwood two marble benches are hidden, behind which the two "Pompeian" fountains – Danaide and Nymph (1850s, architect A. Stackenschneider) – are placed. The alley, leading westwards from the Nymph, circles the picturesque Sand Pond (135 x 57 m), in the centre of which by 1740 a powerful fountain had appeared, designed in the form of "the wooden figure… of a whale." In the late 18th century the fountain became ménager – economical.

Danaide Fountain of the Eastern Marble Bench beside the Great Parterres.
Architect A. Stackenschneider, sculptor I. Vitali. 1850s

Whale Fountain. *Since 2001 the jet of the fountain holds and rolls the gilt ball, "the apple", which is made after models of the 18th century*

Memorable Bench

The bench is placed westwards from the Whale Fountain and presents monument to the younger daughter of Nicholas I – Grand Duchess Alexandra Nikolayevna (1825–44), who died in Petersburg in the year of her marriage with Prince of Hesse-Kassel. Nicholas I immensely suffered from his daughter's death. In her memory he founded the Alexandrine Hospital in Petersburg, built a chapel in Tsarskoe Selo, and in Peterhof he placed this memorable bench with the bust of his daughter (sculptor Ivan Vitali).

Lion Cascade

Northwards from the Memorable Bench the path leads to one more monument of the age of Nicholas I – the Lion Cascade. The cascade first appeared in the late 18th century (the architect Andrei Voronikhin). It got its name because of the bronze figures of lions placed beside it (sculptor Ivan Prokofyev). In 1854–57 Andrei Stackenschneider built the Classical Greek colonnade of granite columns, which are 8 metres high, in the place of the Voronikhin cascade. The twelve marble bowl fountains were placed inside the colonnade between the columns. The Nymph Aganippe Fountain was erected in the centre of it.

Nymph Aganippe Fountain

One of the two
Lion Fountains of the cascade

View of the Marly ensemble from the Golden Hill Cascade. In the background, the Venus Garden

Marly

The Marly ensemble is a park on the eastern border of the Lower Park. It got its name after the royal Marly Residence in the suburbs of Paris. In the row of the Peterhof monuments this is special one as it was constructed in the Petrine age and hasn't had any serious changes since then.

The centre of the ensemble is represented by the refined palace, almost without decoration. It was built on the island between two ponds. The works on the construction of the palace began in 1720 with the building of the ponds, to be more specific, from the Quay Pond (the Great Marly Pond). Later the Sectorial Pond was made. It is divided by three arch bridges, 30 m long each.

Northwards from the palace the small fruit garden (the Venus Garden) is laid out. It was laid out in 1721–24 and protected by the ground bank (about 250 m long) from the Gulf. The bank is supported by the high brick wall with niches. Southwards from the palace the marble Golden Hill Cascade (the Marly Cascade) is placed on the natural terrace. It's one of the most beautiful fountains in Peterhof.

One of the Cloche Fountains in the Bacchus Garden

← *A bird's-eye view of the Marly ensemble*

Sculptures of white marble at the Golden Hill Cascade

The upper landing has an attic with three gilt mascarons erupting water, which is streaming over the twenty-one steps into the figured pool. The attic and the sides of the cascade stairway are decorated with Italian marble sculptures, which replaced the lead gilt ones in 1870. Designed by Michetti, the cascade had been erected by 1722. In 1731–32, the walls of the Cascade steps were faced with gilt copper sheets, sparkling under sunbeams, hence the name – the Golden Hill.

There is a small garden, the Bacchus Garden, in the parterre, in front of the Golden Hill. Its main decoration is the two marble pools 25 m in diameter with the powerful Ménager Fountains constructed by Peter the Great. There are four small Bell (Cloche) Fountains along the border of the Garden. The idea of the fountains belongs to Peter I, who had set the four small fountains by 1724. They were supplied with water from the pipes of the Ménager Fountains. In 1732 the small fountains were decorated with triton figures, which were cast in England in 1721 for the Great Grotto of the Great Cascade.

Western Ménager Fountain

Entrance Hall

Kitchen

Marly Palace

The palace itself has the area of about just 113 square metres and originally, in 1721, was one-storeyed. A year later Peter I ordered to add one more floor. By 1724 the construction of its sixteen rooms had been finished. The smartest rooms are the Entrance Hall, the Dining-Room, the Oak and the Plane Studies and the Bedroom, upholstered with the fabric with refined patterns of pinks and camomiles.

The palace was turned into the museum as early as the mid-18th century, when the rarities from the first wooden "quay" palace were brought here. Now the decoration includes the beautiful furniture of high quality and the then precious porcelain tableware. On the exhibition, are pictures and books of Peter's collection and personal belongings of Peter I.

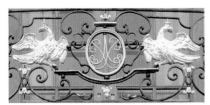

*Balcony railing of the Marly Palace,
with the monogram of Peter I – PP (Peter Primus)*

Icon of Apostles Peter and Paul.
Early 18th century

Oak side-board in the Pantry.
*Delft faience and Chinese and Japanese
porcelain of the 17th – early 18th centuries
are on the shelves*

Dining-Room.
*Italian walnut dining table is in the
centre of the room. 18th century*

**"Portuguese" oak chair in the
Dressing-Room of Peter I.**
*The chair is upholstered
with the cordovan leather
(the leather with the
engraved ornament).
Late 17th – early
18th centuries*

Main Gates of the Upper Garden

Berso Gallery

Upper Garden

The garden serves as a way to the Great Palace and presents a vast (15 ha) French parterre park. The architecture of the park includes fountains, sculptures and small landscape forms: boschetto gardens, berso alleys with pergola arbours, trellises, espaliers and others.

Under Peter I the Upper Garden, "very beautifully situated", according to Bergholz's words, served as the court vegetable and fruit lands. During the years of Empress Anna Ioannovna's reign (1730–40) it was surrounded by the trellis fence; gilt sculptures and tubs with trees were placed along the paths and fountains were erected on the three right-angled pools of the Petrine age and on the two new ones (round, 30 m in diameter). It was the architect Rastrelli who finished the decoration of the garden in 1754–60. He built a high fence on 150 pillars around it, decorated with cartouches and lion masks, and set the gate at the entrance.

Oak Fountain with the sculpture of Putto putting the mask on. Sculptor J. de Rossi. 1809

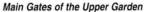

Parterre at the Oak Fountain
White-marble sculptures of the parterre were made by the Paduan master Antonio Bonazza (the son of Giovanni Bonazza, the author of the Adam and Eve Fountains in the Lower Park, pp. 78–79). The sculptures represent the Antique gods – Flora, Zephyrus, the gardener god Vertumnus and his wife, the goddess of fruits, Pomona (1757).

Statue of Zephyrus, the god of the west wind

Central part of the façade of the Great Palace from the side of the Upper Garden

← **Panorama of the Upper Garden.** In the foreground, Apollo Cascade at the Neptune Fountain

Sculpture at the foot of the pedestal of the Neptune Fountain.
In the centre, one of the two riders on the hippocampuses (fantastic sea horses), on the sides of which the puttos on the sea monsters are triumphing

Neptune Fountain

The Neptune Fountain is the main fountain in the Upper Garden. It is set in the pool with the area of 92 x 33 m, constructed in 1721 by the engineer Tuvolkov after Le Blond's drafts.

The present monumental composition with a lot of figures decorated the centre of the pool in the late 18th century. The twenty-tonne bronze creation of the German Baroque was cast in Nuremberg by the foundry master Herold after the models by Ritter, Schweiger, Eisler and Wohlrab in 1668. It had been kept in parts till the 1780s, when Tsesarevitch Paul Petrovitch bought it. When Paul became the Emperor (1796), he ordered to take away the old Neptune and to place the Nuremberg one instead.

Dolphin Fountain in the pool of the Mezheumny ("having no name") Fountain

Under Nicholas I (1825–55) such architects as Joseph Charlemagne, Nicholas Benois and Andrei Benois worked in Peterhof. They were adepts of "historicism", followers of the then popular stylistic "reconstructions." After their designs some new landscape parks were laid out in the place of "vacant lots and groves" around the central ensemble of Peterhof. Those were mainly Alexandria (to the east) and the Colony Park (to the south).

Panorama of the Olgin Pond with a view of the Olgin Pavilion *(to the left)* **and the Tsaritsyn Pavilion** *(to the right)*

Colony Park

The Colony Park was founded in 1838. It got its name after the buildings of the Alexandrovskaya German colony bordering with it. The most part of the territory of the park (29 ha) is occupied by the picturesque artificial reservoir – the Olgin Pond, named after one of the daughters of Nicholas I. The pavilion palaces Tsaritsyn and Olgin were placed on the pond on the two small islands, where originally one could come only by water. They are designed by the architect Andrei Stackenschneider. First, the Tsaritsyn Pavilion, was built as a present of Nicholas I to his wife Alexandra Fiodorovna. The more unpretentious Olgin Pavilion represents a tower in the Toscana style with a gallery and a terrace. It was the Emperor's wedding present to his daughter Olga, who got married with Prince of Württemberg (1847).

← **Peter and Paul Cathedral
in the Colony Park.**
Architect N. Sultanov. 1905

View of the Tsaritsyn Island.
*K. Schulz
after E. Meier's drawing.
Mid-19th century*

Tsaritsyn Pavilion

Parterre Garden by the Tsaritsyn Pavilion

The works on the construction of the palace
and the garden on the Tsaritsyn Island were held
in 1842–44. The author of the design of the
ensemble, Andrei Stackenschneider, supported
Aristotle's thought, who considered that hand-
made landscapes should make the man happy.
Actually, the garden and the palace of the island
had the same aim – that of creation of a peaceful
Antique Mediterranean landscape. Antique
gardens and villas became their prototypes.
On the southern border of the garden the bright-
blue Crystal Column is placed. It was made of
bronze and glass and was presented to Empress
Alexandra Fiodorovna by Prussian King Friedrich
Wilhelm IV (1854).

The landing stage at the palace from the side
of the pond is decorated with sculpture, and the
terrace is fenced by cast-iron railing with vases.
From the side of the garden the inner yard of the
palace is arranged, from where the outer staircase
leads to the first floor of the palace tower into the
study of Nicholas I.

The fountain "The Eagle and the Snake" in the inner yard of the Tsaritsyn Pavilion

Terrace of the Tsaritsyn Pavilion with a view of the Olgin Pond and "Sleeping Nymph" ("Venus") of white marble on the terrace. Sculptor Cincinnato Baruzzi. Mid-19th century

Narcissus Fountain and the white-marble benches in the parterre garden

Interiors of the Tsaritsyn Pavilion

Inside the pavilion is designed to resemble a Pompeian villa. The central place is occupied by the Atrium, painted in the "Pompeian" style and richly decorated with marble. In the centre of the Atrium the marble swimming pool is placed. It has a vase fountain, the jets of which create a small cupola in the marble bowl. There are small bronze copies of famous antique sculptures on the parapets of the pool.

The Atrium is attached by two rooms. The first one is the Oikos (the Drawing-Room), paved with marble. The hall has on the exhibition the splendid Etruscan Service, specially made at the Imperial Porcelain Factory for the Tsaritsyn Pavilion (1844).

The second room is the Exedra (the room with niches) with the furniture from the workshop of Hienrich Gambs. In the niches, semicircular divans and tables with marble and mosaic tabletops and gilt legs (1830s) stands. All the articles of the room are made in the "Pompeian" style.

The doors of the Oikos open to the Dining Room and the Study of Empress Alexandra Fiodorovna. In the Dining-Room the Coral Service is displayed, which as well as the Etruscan one, was specially made at the Imperial Porcelain Factory for the Tsaritsyn Pavilion (1846). The floor of the room is decorated with the original rare ancient Roman mosaics, got by Nicholas I.

Oikos (the Drawing Room)

Cottage Palace →

The Dining-Room

One of the niches of the Exedra (the room with three niches)

Drawing-Room (the ground floor)

Cottage Palace

Nicholas I with the Dog Called Gusar at the Cottage Palace.
E. Botman. 1849

Alexandria is a vast landscape park (the area is 115 ha), which lies eastwards from the central Peterhof ensemble. It is separated from the latter by the high stone wall. The park also partially occupies the seaside low land and partially the high natural terrace. The central building of the park is the Cottage Palace standing on the terrace. It used to be the personal dacha of the wife of Nicholas I, Empress Alexandra Fiodorovna.

The park ensemble also includes the Church of Alexander Nevsky (the Gothic Chapel), standing far westwards from the palace, and the Farm Palace (the dacha of Emperor Alexander II), built on the way to the church. All the buildings are designed in the Gothic style.

The Cottage Palace got its name for it resembles English cottages. Its construction was started in 1826, after the order by the Tsar "in the place of Menshikov's ruins to build a country house, or the so-called 'cottage' with all household rooms and with a park attached."

Dining-Room

Lobby

The works were headed by the elderly Scottish architect Adam Menelaws (about 1750–1831), who arrived in Russia in 1784 and started his career of the Court Architect under Catherine II. The Cottage Palace, with its lyrical mood, resembling English country houses, became the best creation of Menelaws.

The Cottage had been built and decorated by 1829.

The façades of the palace have the Coat-of-Arms of Alexandria under the double-pitched roofs. It was invented by the poet Vasily Zhukovsky: the naked sword with the edge up, passing through the wreath of roses on the blue shield.

The interiors of the Cottage do not have any solemn halls, and the design of its twenty rooms is rich, but functional. It is connected with the private character of the palace, which was not used for grand official receptions. The rooms exhibit the paintings, photographs, graphics, furniture, porcelain, silver, bronze and other articles from the family collection of Nicholas I and Alexandra Fiodorovna. Part of the things appeared under Tsesarevitch Alexander Alexandrovitch (future Alexander III) and his wife Maria Fiodorovna, who owned the Cottage since 1867.

Empress Alexandra Fiodorovna during an equestrian walk.
Decorative bronze sculpture. 1830s (?)

Small Study of Empress Alexandra Fiodorovna

Bay window of the Dining-Room

Carved screen in the Gothic style with the
Coat-of-Arms of Alexandria and stained-glass windows

Study of Empress Maria Fiodorovna.
Designed in 1896–97 in the Art-Nouveau style with the furniture from the famous Saint-Petersburg Meltsers' Factory. The walls are faced with Karelian birch wainscots. The collection of objects of decorative and applied arts contains the glassware of the firms Gallé and the Daum brothers, porcelain trinkets and tableware of the Copenhagen Royal Factory and others.

Small Reception Room. Designed in the "Second Rococo" style in the mid-19th century. The walls are faced with oak wainscots

Porcelain wash-hand-stand from the bedroom of the Grand Duchess Alexandra Nikolayevna, the daughter of Nicholas I

"Rose" window of the Chapel

Gothic Chapel
(The Church of Alexander Nevsky)

This small church in the Gothic style, with the altar consecrated to Alexander Nevsky, was built as a home church of the Imperial family in the early 1830s. The design of the church was created by the Berlin architect Karl Friedrich Schinkel, and the works were headed by the architects Adam Menelaws and Joseph Charlemagne, and the sculptor Vasily Demuth-Malinovsky.

Western portal of the Chapel

Farm Palace

The creation of the palace was started with the building of the pastoral Farm with a row of household buildings not far from the Cottage. It was built by Adam Menelaws. In 1838–39 Andrei Stackenschneider built a two-storeyed house, attached to the Farm, with habitable rooms for the successor to the throne, Alexander Nikolayevitch. By 1859, after a number of reconstructions, the ensemble had turned into the palace, which got the name of the Farm Palace. The family of Alexander II, who had become the Emperor by that time, stayed here in summer. The palace had a playground village for the Emperor children. After the death of Alexander II, his son Alexander III lived in the Tsar's Palace with his family.

View of the Farm Palace in Alexandria. E. Mayer (?)

Alexander III and Empress Maria Fiodorovna with their children Nicholas (future Nicholas II), Georgy, Ksenia, Mikhail and Olga.
Early 1890s

Great Palace. *Plan of the first floor*

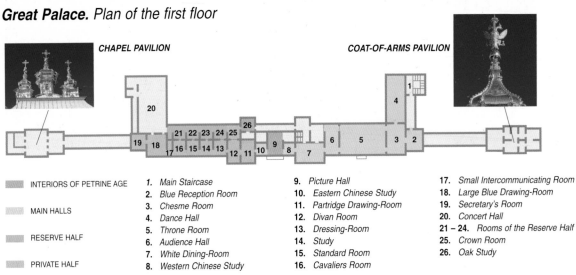

CHAPEL PAVILION **COAT-OF-ARMS PAVILION**

- ▓ INTERIORS OF PETRINE AGE
- ▓ MAIN HALLS
- ▓ RESERVE HALF
- ▓ PRIVATE HALF

1. Main Staircase
2. Blue Reception Room
3. Chesme Room
4. Dance Hall
5. Throne Room
6. Audience Hall
7. White Dining-Room
8. Western Chinese Study
9. Picture Hall
10. Eastern Chinese Study
11. Partridge Drawing-Room
12. Divan Room
13. Dressing-Room
14. Study
15. Standard Room
16. Cavaliers Room
17. Small Intercommunicating Room
18. Large Blue Drawing-Room
19. Secretary's Room
20. Concert Hall
21 – 24. Rooms of the Reserve Half
25. Crown Room
26. Oak Study

Great Cascade. *The scheme of the sculpture placement*

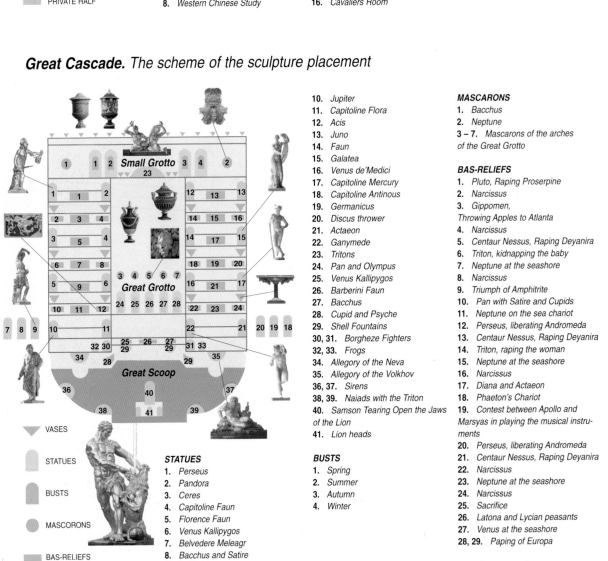

- ▼ VASES
- STATUES
- BUSTS
- MASCORONS
- ▓ BAS-RELIEFS

10. Jupiter
11. Capitoline Flora
12. Acis
13. Juno
14. Faun
15. Galatea
16. Venus de'Medici
17. Capitoline Mercury
18. Capitoline Antinous
19. Germanicus
20. Discus thrower
21. Actaeon
22. Ganymede
23. Tritons
24. Pan and Olympus
25. Venus Kallipygos
26. Barberini Faun
27. Bacchus
28. Cupid and Psyche
29. Shell Fountains
30, 31. Borgheze Fighters
32, 33. Frogs
34. Allegory of the Neva
35. Allegory of the Volkhov
36, 37. Sirens
38, 39. Naiads with the Triton
40. Samson Tearing Open the Jaws of the Lion
41. Lion heads

STATUES
1. Perseus
2. Pandora
3. Ceres
4. Capitoline Faun
5. Florence Faun
6. Venus Kallipygos
7. Belvedere Meleagr
8. Bacchus and Satire
9. Amazon

BUSTS
1. Spring
2. Summer
3. Autumn
4. Winter

MASCARONS
1. Bacchus
2. Neptune
3 – 7. Mascarons of the arches of the Great Grotto

BAS-RELIEFS
1. Pluto, Raping Proserpine
2. Narcissus
3. Gippomen, Throwing Apples to Atlanta
4. Narcissus
5. Centaur Nessus, Raping Deyanira
6. Triton, kidnapping the baby
7. Neptune at the seashore
8. Narcissus
9. Triumph of Amphitrite
10. Pan with Satire and Cupids
11. Neptune on the sea chariot
12. Perseus, liberating Andromeda
13. Centaur Nessus, Raping Deyanira
14. Triton, raping the woman
15. Neptune at the seashore
16. Narcissus
17. Diana and Actaeon
18. Phaeton's Chariot
19. Contest between Apollo and Marsyas in playing the musical instruments
20. Perseus, liberating Andromeda
21. Centaur Nessus, Raping Deyanira
22. Narcissus
23. Neptune at the seashore
24. Narcissus
25. Sacrifice
26. Latona and Lycian peasants
27. Venus at the seashore
28, 29. Paping of Europa

On the 2nd page of the cover:
Peter I and Goddess Minerva.
Artist J. Amiconi. 1730s.